What is
temperature?

Robin Johnson

Crabtree Publishing Company
www.crabtreebooks.com

Author
Robin Johnson

Publishing plan research and development
Sean Charlebois, Reagan Miller
Crabtree Publishing Company

Editors
Reagan Miller, Crystal Sikkens

Proofreader
Kathy Middleton

Photo research
Crystal Sikkens

Design
Ken Wright

**Production coordinator
and prepress technician**
Ken Wright

Print coordinator
Katherine Berti

Illustrations
Katherine Berti: page 9

Photographs
Shutterstock: front and back cover, pages 4, 7, 10 (right), 11 (right),
12, 13, 14, 16, 17, 18 (left and middle), 19 (box), 20
Thinkstock: pages 1, 3, 5, 6, 8, 10 (left), 11 (left), 15, 18 (right),
19 (thermometer), 22

Library and Archives Canada Cataloguing in Publication

Johnson, Robin (Robin R.)
      What is temperature? / Robin Johnson.

(Weather close-up)
Includes index.
Issued also in electronic formats.
ISBN 978-0-7787-0755-4 (bound).--ISBN 978-0-7787-0762-2 (pbk.)

      1. Temperature--Juvenile literature.
I. Title. II. Series: Weather close-up

QC271.4.J64 2012   j536'.5   C2012-904369-9

Library of Congress Cataloging-in-Publication Data

CIP available at Library of Congress

Crabtree Publishing Company

www.crabtreebooks.com   1-800-387-7650

Printed in Hong Kong/092012/BK20120629

**Published in Canada
Crabtree Publishing**
616 Welland Ave.
St. Catharines, Ontario
L2M 5V6

**Published in the United States
Crabtree Publishing**
PMB 59051
350 Fifth Avenue, 59th Floor
New York, New York 10118

**Published in the United Kingdom
Crabtree Publishing**
Maritime House
Basin Road North, Hove
BN41 1WR

**Published in Australia
Crabtree Publishing**
3 Charles Street
Coburg North
VIC 3058

Contents

Changing weather

Weather is what the air and sky are like each day. Weather changes from day to day. On some days, the weather is hot and sunny. Your ice cream melts and drips to the ground before you can eat it! On other days, the weather is cold and cloudy. You shiver and shake and your teeth chatter. Your ice cream stays frozen, but you are too cold to eat it!

Highs and lows

Temperature is an important part of the weather each day. Temperature is how hot or cold the air is. People measure the temperature by using a **thermometer**. When the temperature is high, the weather feels hot. You wear shorts and a t-shirt to stay cool. When the temperature is low, the weather feels cold. You put on your coat, hat, and other warm clothing before you go outside.

Knowing the temperature helps you plan your activities and choose what clothes to wear each day.

Bringing the heat

The Sun gives Earth heat and light. It shines down from the sky and warms the Earth. Without the Sun, the world would be cold and dark. There would be no living things.

You can feel the warmth of the Sun on your skin. If you are not careful, you will get a sunburn!

Climate

Some parts of the world get a lot of Sun all year long. These places have hot **climates**. Climate is the normal weather in an area. Other parts of the world get less Sun. These places have cold climates.

Some places are freezing cold all year long! The animals that live there have thick fur to keep them warm.

Four seasons

Most parts of the world have different **seasons**. A season is a period of time with certain weather and temperatures. There are four seasons. They are winter, spring, summer, and fall. What season is it where you live?

You can have fun in every season of the year! This girl is playing in some leaves in the fall.

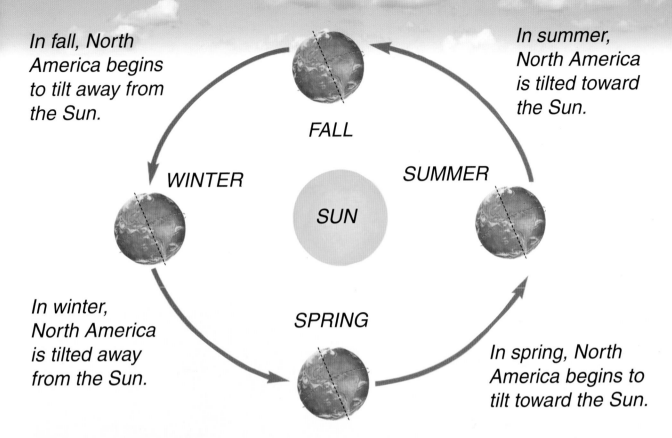

In fall, North America begins to tilt away from the Sun.

In summer, North America is tilted toward the Sun.

FALL

WINTER

SUMMER

SUN

SPRING

In winter, North America is tilted away from the Sun.

In spring, North America begins to tilt toward the Sun.

The reason for seasons

Earth circles around the Sun once each year. As Earth moves, some places on Earth are closer to the Sun at certain times of the year. They get a lot of sunlight and warm seasons. When places are turned away from the Sun, they get less sunlight and cooler seasons.

Take your temperature!

People use thermometers to measure temperature. A thermometer is a tool that shows how hot or cold the air is. Some thermometers have colored liquid inside them. The liquid rises or falls based on the temperature of the air. What temperature is this thermometer showing? Read the number at the top of the red liquid to find out!

By degrees

Some thermometers measure temperature in **degrees** Fahrenheit (°F). Other thermometers measure temperature in degrees Celsius (°C). Many thermometers show both Fahrenheit and Celsius.

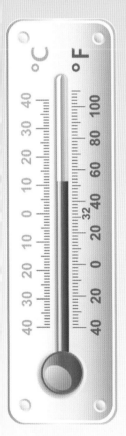

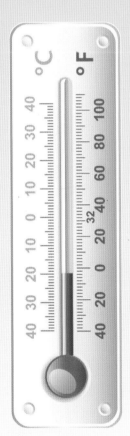

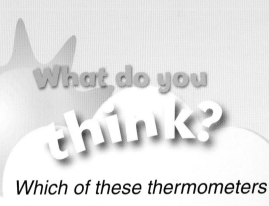

Which of these thermometers shows a temperature you would see in summer?

11

Blowing hot or cold

Each season has different temperatures. In some parts of the world, winter is freezing cold. Temperatures can drop below 32°F (0°C). Then it is cold enough to snow! In spring, the temperatures rise and the snow melts. The weather is warm and rainy. Flowers and other plants begin to grow.

Keep your cool

In some places, summer brings high temperatures and hot, sunny weather. The temperature can climb to 100°F (38°C) or more! People go to the beach or swim in pools to stay cool. In fall, the temperatures start to drop. The weather gets cool and windy. Soon it will be winter again.

What do you think?

Can you guess which seasons the pictures on these pages are showing? How can you tell what the temperature is?

Clouds, wind, and water

Temperatures change each season, but they also change from day to day. Clouds, wind, and water can all make the weather feel hotter or colder. Clouds block some of the Sun's rays from heating up Earth, so the temperature is cooler on cloudy days. On windy days, the temperature feels cooler than it really is. The more the wind blows, the colder it feels!

In the air

Some days, the air is **humid**. Humid air has a lot of **water vapor** in it. On a hot day, humid air makes the temperature feel hotter than it really is. On a cold day, humid air makes the weather feel colder and damp.

This dog is trying to get cool in the shade. It is a hot dog!

Heat waves and cold days

Sometimes the temperature can be too hot to handle! A **heat wave** is a long period of time with very hot, humid weather. Heat waves can make people and animals sick. They can also damage crops and roads.

During a heat wave, you should rest in the shade or stay indoors where there is air conditioning.

Come in from the cold!

Very cold temperatures can also be harmful. Long periods of freezing cold weather can cause frostbite. **Frostbite** is an injury to a person's skin. Cold weather can also cause water pipes in buildings to freeze and burst.

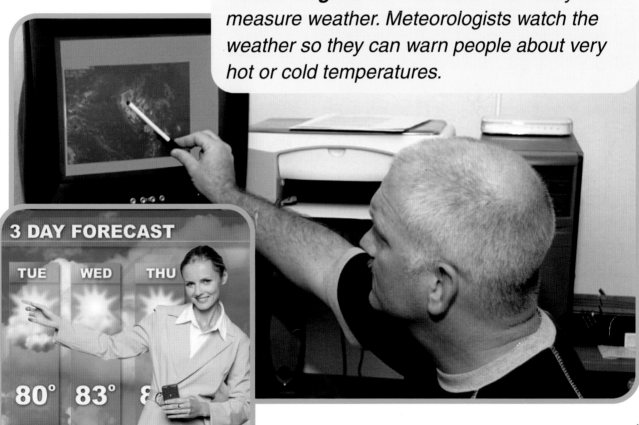

Meteorologists are scientists who study and measure weather. Meteorologists watch the weather so they can warn people about very hot or cold temperatures.

3 DAY FORECAST

TUE   WED   THU

80°   83°   8

Make a thermometer box!

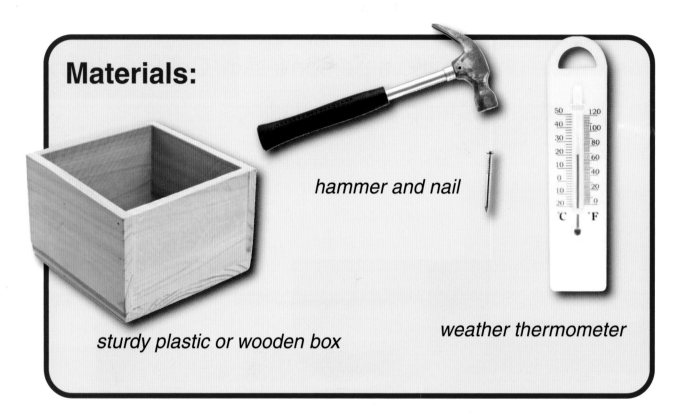

Materials:

hammer and nail

sturdy plastic or wooden box

weather thermometer

Follow these steps to make a **thermometer box**.
A thermometer box is a container that protects an
outdoor thermometer from the Sun, rain, wind, and
other weather.

What to do:

1. Ask an adult to hammer a nail to the inside bottom of the box.

2. Put the thermometer on the nail.

3. Turn the box on its side so the thermometer hangs on the back wall of the box.

4. Find a flat, shady spot outside to put the box. You can rest the back of the box against a building or fence to help keep it in place.

5. Read the thermometer. Try to check it at the same time each day.

6. Write down the temperature in degrees Fahrenheit or degrees Celsius.

What do you think?

What happens if you put your thermometer box in the Sun? Does the temperature go up or down? Why does it change?

Journals and graphs

Check the temperature on your thermometer each day and record the **data**, or information, in a **weather journal**. A weather journal is a notebook for writing and drawing pictures about the weather.

Show your stuff!

You can use the data in your weather journal to make a graph. A graph is a picture that shows and compares information. Your graph could show how hot or cold it was at a certain time each day of the week. It could also show the change in temperature during a single day. What else could a temperature graph show?

This line graph shows the changes in temperature from day to day.

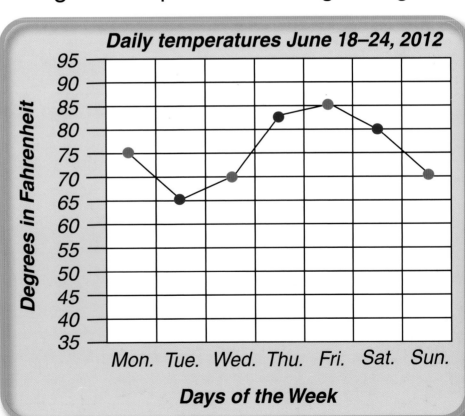

Daily temperatures June 18–24, 2012

Degrees in Fahrenheit

Days of the Week

Graphing temperature

Rachel used her weather journal to record the change in temperature throughout the day on Saturday, February 4, 2012. She used this data to create a line graph. Look at Rachel's graph. What time of the day had the highest temperature? When was the lowest temperature?

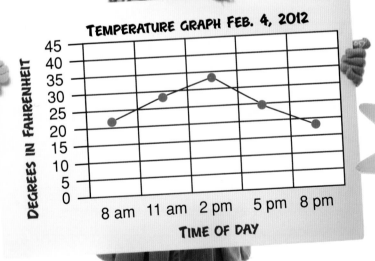

TEMPERATURE GRAPH FEB. 4, 2012

DEGREES IN FAHRENHEIT

8 am   11 am   2 pm   5 pm   8 pm

TIME OF DAY

What do you think?

Why do you think Rachel's graph showed the high and low temperatures at these times?

22

Find out more

Books

Changing Seasons (Nature's Changes) by Bobbie Kalman and Kelley MacAulay. Crabtree Publishing Company, 2005.

The Weather (Now we know about) by Mike Goldsmith. Crabtree Publishing Company, 2009.

Temperature (Measuring the Weather) by Alan Rodgers. Heinemann Raintree, 2007.

What is climate? (Big Science Ideas) by Bobbie Kalman. Crabtree Publishing Company, 2012.

Websites

Weather Wiz Kids
www.weatherwizkids.com/weather-temperature.htm

Fossweb Air and Weather Module
www.fossweb.com/modulesK-2/AirandWeather/index.html

United States Search and Rescue Task Force: Predicting Weather
www.ussartf.org/predicting_weather.htm

Glossary

Note: Some boldfaced words are defined where they appear in the book.

climate (KLAHY-mit) noun The weather that an area has had for a long period of time

degree (dih-GREE) noun A unit of measurement for temperature

humid (HYOO-mid) adjective Describing air that has a lot of water in it and feels damp

meteorologist (mee-tee-uh-ROL-uh-jist) noun A scientist who studies and measures weather

season (SEE-zuhn) noun A period of time with certain temperatures and weather

temperature (TEHM-per-a-chur) noun How cold or warm the air is

thermometer (THUR-mom-itur) noun A tool that measures the temperature of air and water

water vapor (WOT-er VEY-per) noun Water in the air that you cannot see

A noun is a person, place, or thing. An adjective is a word that tells you what something is like.

Index